W9-ADV-554

IN MEMORY OF MARION MOREHOUSE CUMMINGS

Eve Triem's poetry has been published in the volumes *Parade of Doves* and *Poems* as well as in many magazines and anthology collections. A resident of Seattle, she has lectured on poetry from coast to coast.

E. E. Cummings

OBEDIENT to the world spirit of change, in the early decades of the twentieth century a group of notable poets, by diverging from traditional practices, transformed American poetry. The most thorough "smasher of the logicalities" among them was a transcendentalist: one who views nature as a state of becoming rather than as a stasis and who believes that the imaginative faculty in man can perceive the natural world directly. He was also a troubadour who said: "enters give/ whose lost is his found/ leading love/ whose heart is her mind." He was not only poet but novelist, playwright, and painter. In following his vision he roused hostility in academic critics and readers, apparently repelled by his idiosyncratic typographical and stylistic devices, but he was from the beginning admired by his fellow innovators, William Carlos Williams, Marianne Moore, Ezra Pound, and T. S. Eliot — and eventually he won the esteem of his critics.

"I am someone," remarked E. E. Cummings late in his career, "who proudly and humbly affirms that love is the mystery-of-mysteries . . . that 'an artist, a man, a failure' is . . . a naturally and miraculously whole human being . . . whose only happiness is to transcend himself, whose every agony is to grow." In a world oriented to dehumanized power, transcendentalism is a synonym for absurdity. Cummings recognized this early. In an address at his Harvard commencement in 1915, he had said, "we are concerned with the natural unfolding of sound tendencies. That the conclusion is, in a particular case, *absurdity*, does not in any way impair the value of the experiment, so long as we are dealing with sincere effort." The manifesto he issued then was that of one man to himself. He would experiment, and he would not fear being absurd; he would use the absurdity principle to the limit of its usefulness. As he worked at his trade of wordsmith, the implications of what he had said in 1915 were clarified in a remarkable stream of poems. From the start he used absurdity to leaven the commonplace, to startle readers into "listening" instead of merely hearing. In his later years he discovered a new significance in the concept: experimental living and the practice of his craft had redefined absurdity; it came to mean the truth of earthly living and a promise of eternity.

Edward Estlin Cummings, son of the Reverend Edward Cummings (lecturer at Harvard and Unitarian minister) and of Rebecca Haswell Clarke Cummings, was born at Cambridge, Massachusetts, on October 14, 1894. His parents had been brought together by their mutual friend William James. Dr. Cummings was a woodsman, a photographer, an actor, a carpenter, an artist – and talented in all that he undertook. Mrs. Cummings was a shy woman who overcame conventional influences to respond joyously and effectively to life. The son was educated in public schools and at Harvard University where he received an A.B., *magna cum laude,* and an M.A. for English and classical studies.

While Cummings was in graduate school he helped to found the Harvard Poetry Society. He and some of his friends in the society put together *Eight Harvard Poets* (published in 1917). In it, by a printer's error, according to one story, Cummings' name and the "I's" as well were set in lowercase letters. He seized upon this as a device congenial to him and later had "e. e. cummings" legalized as his signature.

After Harvard, Cummings went to New York. In this city he held his first and only job, three months with P. F. Collier & Son, Inc., mail-order booksellers. He was twenty-one at the time. In mid-1917 he went to France to serve as a volunteer ambulance driver. There he was interned for a minor military offense—what happened was that he refused to say he hated Germans; instead, with typical Cummings care for precision, he repeated: "I like the French." From his experiences at La Fertè Macé (a detention camp) he accumulated material for his documentary "novel," *The Enormous Room* (1922), one of the best war books by an American.

Upon his release, he returned to the United States, but when the war ended he went back to Paris—this time to study art. He made the acquaintance of the poet Louis Aragon and of Picasso and their circle of poets and painters; he became friendly with many visiting writers such as Archibald MacLeish and Ezra Pound. On arriving back in New York in 1924 he found himself a celebrity—for his documentary novel and for *Tulips and Chimneys* (1923), his first book of poems. The next year he won the *Dial* Award for "distinguished service to American Letters." A roving assignment from *Vanity Fair* in 1926 permitted him to go abroad again, where he established a routine he was to follow most of his life: he painted in the afternoons and wrote at night.

From his experiences in the two cities he loved, New York and Paris, came the material for scintillating or extravagant essays on burlesque, the circus, modern art, and the foibles of the day, later collected into *A Miscellany* (1958) and *A Miscellany, Revised* (1965). He wrote forewords to books and brochures for art exhibits, and he sold sketches and paintings. Three volumes of poetry appeared in quick succession: *&* (*And*) and *XLI Poems* in 1925, *Is 5* in 1926. The play *Him*, a phantasmagoria in 21 scenes, which was a forerunner of what is now called the Theater of the Absurd, was published in 1927 and produced by the Provincetown Players in 1928 and was acclaimed by avant-garde critics. In 1931 he published a collection of drawings and paintings,

CIOPW, which took its title from the initial letters of the materials used: charcoal, ink, oil, pencil, watercolor. In that same year came *W* (*ViVa*), a thick book of poems. A travel journal published in 1933, *Eimi* (I Am), recorded his revulsion against an even more "enormous room" than the military detention camp: the collectivized Soviet Union.

After 1930, although Cummings continued to travel abroad, he divided most of his time between a studio apartment in Greenwich Village, at 4 Patchin Place, and the family farm at Silver Lake, New Hampshire. This yearly contact with New England soil occasioned one of his finest poem-portraits: "rain or hail/sam done/ the best he kin/ till they digged his hole." A similar earthy wisdom is in a poem that may be a comment on himself: "my specialty is living said/ a man(who could not earn his bread/ because he would not sell his head)."

Because he had in common with T. S. Eliot not only a New England Unitarian background but also cosmopolitan traits, it is stimulating to observe the differences between them. Eliot became a British citizen. Cummings, responding to French art, always admiring the French civilization, nonetheless spent most of his life in the United States. He was a goldfinch needing a native tree to sing from. Through the years, from his perch, he continued to pour forth his songs: *No Thanks* (1935), *50 Poems* (1940), *1 x 1* (*One Times One*, 1944), *Xaipe* (1950). A *Collected Poems* appeared in 1938. The ballet *Tom* was published in 1935 and the plays *Anthropos* and *Santa Claus* were published in 1944 and 1946.

Honors and rewards came with frequency—now. In 1950, for "great achievement," he was given the Fellowship of the Academy of American Poets. In 1952 he was invited to give the Norton Lectures at Harvard (published as *I: Six Nonlectures* in 1953), an urbane but lively analysis of the Cummings quest to discover

"Who as a writer am I?" These lectures could have been subtitled "And who as a person are you?" because — like Walt Whitman with his phrases addressed to future generations who would cross on Brooklyn Ferry — Cummings was always reaching out from the persona, the neutral "i," to the "you" out there. In 1955 he received a special citation from the National Book Awards for *Poems 1923–1954* (1954) and in 1957 he received both the Bollingen Prize for Poetry and the Boston Arts Festival Poetry Award. A year later the last of his poetry collections to appear during his lifetime was published, *95 Poems.* Cummings the painter was also honored: he had one-man shows in 1944 and 1949 at the American-British Art Centre, and in 1945 and 1959 at the Rochester Memorial Gallery. His wide-ranging interest in the visual arts was reflected in *Adventures in Value* (1962) on which he collaborated with his third wife, photographer Marion Morehouse.

Cummings died on September 3, 1962, in New Hampshire. He left a manuscript of poetry published the following year as *73 Poems.*

"The artist's country is inside him," said Cummings. This was another way of saying that he would abide only by the laws of his own mind. His formalities — the literary devices he developed — were intended to show how the outer appearance reinforces the inner vision. His disordered syntax and typographical disarrangements were intended, not to bewilder, but to heighten the understanding. He described what he was trying to do in the 1926 Foreword to *Is 5*: "my theory of technique, if I have one, is very far from original; nor is it complicated. I can express it in fifteen words, by quoting The Eternal Question And Immortal Answer of burlesk, viz. 'Would you hit a woman with a child? — No, I'd hit her with a brick.' Like the burlesk comedian, I am abnormally fond of that precision which creates movement." One of his methods to achieve this was tmesis (the separation of parts of words by intervening words). It became almost like a signature for him. As Karl Shapiro put it in his *Essay on Rime,* Cummings was concerned with the "Integers of the word, the curve of 'e',/ Rhythm of 'm', astonishment of 'o'/ And their arranged derangement." By the analysis of words into their parts, both syllables and individual letters, and by considered use of space and punctuation marks, as well as by "arranged derangement," Cummings hoped to extend meaning beyond traditional limits.

Cummings used space in his typographical rhetoric to indicate tempo of reading: single words may have spaces within them to force the reader to weigh each syllable, as in "can dy lu/ minous"; or words may be linked, as in "eddieandbill," to convey the act of boys running. A comma may be used where a period is expected, within a poem or at the end of it, to produce a pause for the reader to imagine what the next action might be. Or commas, colons, and semicolons may be used within a word to arouse new sensations and intuitions. In examining the poem beginning "as if as" (*No Thanks*) the reader disentangles from the typography the idea that it is a poem about sunrise. But it is not like other accounts of sunrise, nor, probably, does it reflect the reader's own experience. Toward the end of the poem the word "itself" is fractured into "it:s;elf." The "s" suggests the sun as well as the viewer. "Elf," relating to an earlier phrase, "moon's al-down," is a hint, in this instance, of the supernatural impact of dawn. The daily sun is no longer a habit but a miracle. In a later work (Number 48 in *73 Poems*), the word "thrushes" is divided into "t,h;r:u;s,h;e:s" so that the reader may perceive, with the poet, the individual sleepy birds gripping a branch at moonrise and, by implication, the transcendental relationship between all living things. Of the exclamation point beginning the first poem in

50 Poems, "!blac," Cummings himself said that it might be called an emphatic "very"; the unpronounceable "?" and ")" are often similarly used. To focus the reader's attention a capital letter may be thrust into the middle of a word. In the opening poem of *No Thanks* capitals are used to imitate the roundness of the moon and to imply the eternity of the circle:

mOOn Over tOwns mOOn
whisper
less creature huge grO
pingness

In "i will be" (*And*) the word "SpRiN,k,LiNg" is manipulated to make a visual representation of sunlight filtering through wing feathers. In this poem, too, a parenthesis is used in the middle of the word "wheeling" to place simultaneously before the reader's mind the flutter of the pigeons and their effect on the sunlight:

whee(:are,SpRiN,k,LiNg an in-stant with sunLight
t h e n) l -
ing . . .

Cummings made varied use of parentheses: for an interpolated comment or to split or combine words as a guide to his thought. Frequently they occur, in poem-parables, to clarify the relationship between two sentences that run simultaneously through the poem. In "go(perpe)go," published in *No Thanks,* we have a typical Cummings juxtaposition. The parenthetical sentence is a surrealist collection of "perpetual adventuring particles" describing the action of a disturbed ant heap and an anteater getting his dinner. The sentence outside the parenthesis, "go to the ant, thou anteater," is an allusion to Proverbs 6:6: "Go to the ant, thou sluggard." The poem is description and social comment, disguised as a joke. Critic Norman Friedman analyzed it succinctly: "Cummings is satirizing a certain kind of worldly and prudential wisdom. The ant's activity represents for Cummings merely busy work rather than a model of industry, and he who is advised to 'go to the ant' is the one creature who can possibly profit from such a visit — the anteater. In thus reducing the proverb to its simply 'realistic' aspects — by refusing to make the metaphorical transference intended — Cummings deflates the whole implied point of view."

Some of Cummings' poems utilize the "visual stanza" in which lines are arranged in reference, not to rhyme and meter, but to a shape reflecting the poet's thought. This kind of typographical design, with poems contrived in the form of roses, diamonds, and hourglass figures, was in fashion during the Elizabethan age and continued to be used in the seventeenth century. With changes in taste and technical practice in the last two centuries, this device fell into disuse, although it has been revived occasionally as when Lewis Carroll used it for his mouse's "long and sad tale." More recently it appeared in the *Calligrammes* of Guillaume Apollinaire and in the "quaint" patterning of Dylan Thomas' poem "Vision and Prayer." However, the visual appearance of Cummings' poems can be largely accounted for by his interest in contemporary art forms, rather than by influence from other writers. From artists like Picasso who were bringing new vitality to painting, he learned the effectiveness of distorting lines and reshaping masses; and he juxtaposed words as they did the pigments (in John Peale Bishop's apt phrasing) — to bring perception of things into sharper focus. Cummings specifically disclaimed any stylistic influence from Apollinaire's mimetic typography, and as Gorham B. Munson observed very early, Cummings' typographical design, unlike that of the *Calligrammes,* reinforces the literary content of his poems. Some of Cummings' poems are designed to be read vertically; in others, stanzaic structures are balanced for mass, as are certain colors in painting. Effective examples of Cummings' use of the visual stanza are the poem "!blac" and the ironic dedication to *No Thanks,* which lists in the shape of a wineglass all the publishers who had rejected the manuscript. In *XLI Poems* there is a poem, "little tree," that visually suggests a Christmas tree, and another that on the page resembles smoke puffing out of a locomotive:

```
the
   sky
      was
can dy lu
minous
```

Another important device by which Cummings intended to enlarge the reader's comprehension was word coinage. He kept already existing root words, joining to them new affixes. In such compounded words the prefixes are familiar enough, but his use of the suffixes *-ly, -ish, -est, -ful* and adverbs (such as *less*) in unexpected combinations, a dimension natural to classical and romance languages, produces in English an intensifying of perception. Introduce one or two of these words—*riverly, nowly, downwardishly, birdfully, whichful, girlest, skylessness, onlying, laughtering,* etc.—into a verse of recognizable words and the reader has to explore possibilities in a creative way. In reading creatively a phrase like "on stiffening greenly air" he will cross the threshold of transcendence. Articles and particles were rearranged by Cummings for the same purpose—"some or if where." One part of speech may be used for another as in the first line of a much-anthologized poem from *And,* "Spring is like a perhaps hand." The charm of this line is due in large part to the use of an adverb where an adjective is expected, to emphasize the tentative nature of springtime. This is reinforced by an image of the window dresser who moves things and changes things "without breaking anything," in contrast to the destructions of winter.

In all of these ways Cummings broke language from its conventionalized mold; it became a nourishing soil through which "faces called flowers float out of the ground" (*Xaipe*). Cummings' virtuosity was directed to capture in words what the painter gets on canvas and what children, violently alive in response to objects and seasons, display in their street games. His poems are alive on the page, as he told the printer when he instructed him not to interfere with the "arrangement." Any change would be an injury to living tissue. In discontinuous poems he tried to pin down the "illuminated moment," to ransom from oblivion the fleeting present, in words seasonal, contemporary, and timeless—like a writer of haiku. To get at the realities, Cummings smashed the logicalities, an idea in harmony with Oriental art and philosophy, with which he had acquaintance as shown by a quotation from the Tao that appears near the end of *Eimi*: "he who knoweth the eternal is comprehensive . . . therefore just; just, therefore a king; a king, therefore celestial; celestial, therefore in Tao; in Tao, therefore enduring." Cummings' perpetual concern with transcendental ideas led to the shining leaps on the page that make his work unique.

One needs to remember, however, that this innovating poet was practiced in conventional Western literary tradition. The young Cummings learned from Elizabethan song and eighteenth-century satire, as well as from the Pindaric ode. He was rooted in the same soil as Thoreau, Emerson, and Emily Dickinson. Intermittently he read Aeschylus, Homer, and the French troubadours—as evidenced by his quotations in the *Six Nonlectures.* He cut his literary teeth on the strict rules of villanelle, roundel, and ballade royale. Nonetheless his genius led him to quite different patterns: a poem in *ViVa,* for example, records phonetically not only a conversation but a revelation of the hearts of lost men: "oil tel duh woil doi sez/ dooyah unnurs tanmih eesez pullih nizmus tash,oi/ dough un giv uh shid oi sez. Tom." The emphasis is deliberate and made with care.

Cummings said that Josiah Royce (who appears in one of the poem-portraits) directed his attention to Dante Gabriel Rossetti, especially to Rossetti's sonnets, and that made him a sonneteer. Certainly Cummings wrote some of the finest sonnets of our century: celebrating love, savagely ridiculing human stupidity, and recording his pilgrimage to the transcendental. From the somewhat conventional, Cummings' sonnets developed, as Theodore Spencer has said, to achieve "specific gravity." Yet the only discernible influence of the pre-Raphaelite school is in the early lyrics and might as easily have been been picked up direct from a reading of the sonnets of Dante. There is internal evidence that Shakespeare was the dynamic influence in his sonnet-making: sensory details, the absence of hypocrisy, even the rhythm of the snap at the end, as in a couplet from "being to timelessness as it's to time" in *95 Poems*: "—do lovers love?Why then to heaven with hell./ Whatever sages say and fools,all's well." In an interview with Harvey Breit in 1950 Cummings said: "Today so-called writers are completely unaware of the thing which makes art what it is. You can call it nobility or spirituality, but I should call it intensity. Sordid is the opposite. . . . Shakespeare is never sordid . . . because his poetry was the most intense."

Cummings' experimentation was clearly within Western literary tradition, as was Eliot's, but, finally, whatever he did resulted in poems that could not have been written by anyone else. He has had no successful imitators. And because of its nature Cummings' work cannot be held within the bounds of conventional literary analysis. The critic must stretch his own powers to find the significant new insights waiting to be revealed by this poet's language in action. What is required is "intelligence functioning at intuitional velocity"—Cummings used the phrase to characterize a work of the sculptor Lachaise but it admirably describes the approach a perceptive critic-reader must take to Cummings' writing.

For a study of Cummings' philosophy and of his devices to achieve art in motion and at a peak of excitement, the play *Him,* called by the critic Edmund Wilson "the outpouring of an intelligence, a sensibility, and an imagination of the very first dimension," is especially useful.

The action is divided between "exterior" and "interior" happenings that develop the love story of a man and the predicament of an artist. The satirical exterior scenes are presented before a garish curtain like that used in carnival shows. The deliberate lack of a third dimension is one of the poet's "absurdities"; it symbolizes the "unworld." The curtain and the parodies of circus and burlesque in the play's action reflect his interest in folk amusements. The interior scenes explore the psyche of the creative temperament. Connecting the two phases is the chorus: the three Fates, Atropos, Clotho, Lachesis. They are disguised as the Misses Weird and are nicknamed "Stop," "Look," and "Listen." They sit with their backs to the audience, rocking and knitting, as they swap a nonsensical version of backfence talk and advertising slogans. The stage directions integrate the themes and devices of the play.

In the complex design of *Him,* described by one commentator as "a play of lucid madness and adventurous gaiety," Cummings sets up a confrontation: man, a social being, versus the artist. In the *Six Nonlectures* he repeats: "Nobody else can be alive for you; nor can you be alive for anybody else. . . . There's the artist's responsibility . . ." Yeats knew this human instinct to fulfill strenuous conditions for the sake of an ideal: writing of the Irish playwright J. M. Synge, he said, ". . . to come out from under the shadow of other men's minds . . . to be utterly oneself: that is all the Muses care for." At first glance Yeats's statement seems callous but when it is illustrated in the creative life it leads to service for the community. In the poems beginning "i sing of Olaf glad and big" (*ViVa*) and "a man who had fallen among thieves" (*Is 5*), Cummings is urging awake the sleeping conscience of his fellows. And in *Him* Cummings develops a metaphor, found with varying emphasis in his poetry, that strikingly illustrates his view. The artist is likened to a circus performer who sits astride three chairs stacked one on top of the other and balanced on a high wire. He explains to his lover, "Me," that the three chairs are three facts: "I am an Artist, I am a Man, I am a Failure."

The label on the top chair, "Failure," is disconcerting but acceptable when the reader becomes familiar with the paradoxes of Cummings' vocabulary. To distinguish true accomplishment from the disappointing successes of the salesman-politician-warmongering world, he uses words that for him state the ultimate emptiness of the prizes the crowd pursues and often captures. Throughout Cummings' poems occur the words *failure, nothing, nobody, zero,* and the prefixes *non-* and *un-*. They are also scattered through the prose of *The Enormous Room* and *Eimi*. By these negatives he separated his ideals from the pleasures of a conformist world and showed his condemnation of "mobs" and "gangs" and his concern for the individual. The phrase "you and i" dominates his response to relationships: lovers, mother and child, a man and a city, a man and a tree.

The other two "chairs" of *Him* have a subordinate but vital function in the metaphor. The experiences of the man are limited to the senses until they are fused with the perceptions of the artist. It is from the artist and his transcendental realizations that the reader or viewer learns to distinguish the genuine from the pinchbeck. The artist is also dependent on the report from his five senses to actualize his ideas. So Cummings found spiritualities in "facts" and celebrated them in his poems of love and compassion. The significance that Cummings assigned to "failure" is further evident in a sonnet from *Is 5*, "if i have made, my lady, intricate/ imperfect various things . . ." And a study of the Foreword to *Is 5* will reveal affirmations of the themes of *Him*: that the poet knows he is "competing" with reality and therefore "failure" is predestined. What is increasingly noticeable in the play and in the volumes of poems that follow it is the changing concept of love and the frank presentation of the artist's self-doubt. He insists on finding out who he is before he can be either artist or lover. Cummings' belief that the artist's total attentiveness to an object or subject should result in simultaneity for his audience—which was also the aim of the Imagist movement in poetry and of Cubism in painting—was not completely realizable. He therefore began to think of art as a series of mirrors reflecting the "object" in various lights and not as the thing-in-itself. So, with a sense of the "awful responsibility" of the poet, he regarded his extraordinary successes in putting on the page a flying bird, a grasshopper, a falling leaf as "failures" and called himself a nonhero.

The falling leaf poem is the first of the *95 Poems*. It is not a complete sentence and there are only four words. The form has the narrowness of a needle. In a time when novels tell no story and music is not melodic—relatively speaking—this pictogram brings new insights, which have been perceptively set forth by Norman Friedman and Barry A. Marks in their critical studies of Cummings; their lead is followed here.

Each of the first four lines has but one consonant and one vowel: two *l*'s, three *a*'s, one *e*, and two *f*'s. This suggests the fluttering pattern of a falling leaf. The next line, treated as a stanza, is a double *l*, extending meaning as the reader waits for the necessary completion. The poem ends on a shifting note which accentuates the import of "alone," "one," and "oneliness" (defined as "own").

l(a

le
af
fa

ll

s)
one
l

iness

The mind of the reader seizes the two ideas: loneliness and the parenthetical interjection of the fall of a leaf. In splitting "loneliness" Cummings shows by variations on a word blurred by indiscriminate use that it is, as Marks noted, "quite a singular word." Cummings strips the sheath from the ordinary, and the extraordinary is revealed. The "le/ af/ fa/ ll" involves both sound and visual values; the musical relation echoes the meaning emerging from "le" and "af."

The *l* in "leaf" repeats the first *l* in "loneliness" and helps the reader keep in mind simultaneously the material inside and outside the parentheses. His old typewriter played an important role here in Cummings' idea of form as it affects thought: in the first line *l* can be either the digit "one" or the letter "el." A parenthesis separating it from *a* suggests that while the idea of doubling up on "oneness" is attractive, it is not plausible. Following the trail of the parenthesis, the reader discovers a "verse" that reinforces the necessity that *l* be "el" in the fourth stanza. The word "one" and an apparent digit reflect back to the initial *l* and in their interplay the digit vanishes into the letter.

The reader is pleased with his success in working out the

"puzzle"; casually he has participated in the dance of the poet's mind. Then he arrives at the last line, "iness." The isolation and the desolation of the individual, the I alone with the I, be it a leaf or a man, have been established. Forgotten are the secondary ideas of oneness with the universe or the intimations of autumn: the reader now knows he has misunderstood the form if he accepted it as a needle stitching together all created things. However, as Henry James asserted by implication in *The Wings of the Dove,* the tragic element is art and art is delight. Yet another idea is added to the possibles of interpretation: man's unhappy isolation comes from self-loving activities and trivial goals. Self-forgetfulness is the reward of the disciplined athlete and of the artist, with the result an unblemished performance. The ever-evolving devices of Cummings are a witness to his profoundly moral nature in conflict with an imperfect world, and to his vision that it *could* be perfected.

The "puzzle" of the following lines from *No Thanks* is similarly rewarding to the reader willing to work it out:

r-p-o-p-h-e-s-s-a-g-r
who
a)s w(e loo)k
upnowgath
PPEGORHRASS
eringint(o-
aThe):l
eA
!p:
S a

The poet, through spacings of word and letter and the unorthodox use of capitals, presents a grasshopper living in his muscles. At first he is invisible, coming from the grass to us only in the sounds reverberating from earth or pebbles. But as Lloyd Frankenberg pointed out in his study of modern poetry, *Pleasure Dome*: "These sounds—some soft, some loud, some intermittent—are rearrangements of his name; just as he rearranges himself to rub forewing and hind leg together. Then he 'leaps!' clear so that we see him, 'arriving to become, rearrangingly, grasshopper.'" The reader has been, briefly, the grasshopper and that has extended his capacity for being alive. Note that in this poem Cummings used a device resembling Cubistic painting: "r-p-o-p-h-e-s-s-a-g-r" and "PPEGORHRASS" and ".gRrEaPsPhOs" (which appears after the lines quoted above) record the "realization" of experiences that he wished to share with his readers.

In other poems which demonstrate his delight in the natural world, Cummings often used mimicry. Cummings had a talent like that of the Greek comic playwright Aristophanes, who in his oft-quoted line "Brekekekéx koáx koáx" sought to reproduce the sound of frogs. A similar mimicry is found in such unlikely Cummings poems as the colloquial "buncha hardboil guys from duh A.C. fulla" (*ViVa*) and "joggle i think will do it although the glad" (*Tulips and Chimneys*). In a punning poem, "applaws)" (*One Times One*), the "paw" is a kind of mimicry and a reminder that fundamentally we are animals.

Another aspect of the "creaturely" life that interested Cummings is to be found in his poems about horses, those animals now vanishing from sight, except in parades or circuses. In the lines below from a poem in *No Thanks* the scene is set by "crazily seething of this/ raving city screamingly street." What opens the windows to be "sharp holes in dark places" is the light from flowers. And what do the "whichs" and "small its," the half-alive, half-asleep people see?

what a proud dreamhorse pulling(smoothloomingly)through
(stepp)this(ing)crazily seething of this
raving city screamingly street wonderful

flowers And o the Light thrown by Them opens

sharp holes in dark places paints eyes touches hands with new-

ness and these startled whats are a(piercing clothes thoughts kiss
-ing wishes bodies)squirm-of-frightened shy are whichs small
its hungry for Is for Love Spring thirsty for happens
only and beautiful

Through the raucous sounds of a city street a horse is pulling a load of flowers. In that setting his movements have a grace such as is found in dreams. The horse establishes his reality as we watch him "stepp . . . ing"—the poet has plowed with horses his family's fields; he has watched milk wagons in the city. However, as Lloyd Frankenberg has suggested, the horse, "whose feet almost walk air," brings to mind Pegasus. That wingèd steed of the Muses is associated in legend with Hippocrene, the fountain of inspiration, which supposedly sprang from the earth at a blow from his forehoof. In one legend the Greek hero Bellerophon, with the aid of Pegasus, slew the Chimaera, a ravaging beast. Then he tried to fly to heaven, thereby offending the gods, and fell to earth. A poet is often trying to fly and often he fails. So we come back to the name that Cummings gave himself, "nonhero."

In another city sonnet, from *And* ("my sonnet is A light goes on in"), we meet the dray horses that sleep upstairs in a tenement stable. "Ears win-/ k funny stable. In the morning they go out in pairs." Implied in the poet's words is the ancient horse sacrifice to the sun, to encourage the sun to rise again. So the sonnet comes to a climax on a line of life and beauty: "They pull the morning out of the night." There is the same fidelity to sensory perception in poems that include references to rain: "the rain's/ pearls singly-whispering" (from "the moon is hiding in," *Tulips and Chimneys*) and "i have found what you are like/ the rain" (*And*).

The opening lines of an early poem, from *Tulips and Chimneys,* show both Cummings' delight in the natural world and his ability to respond freshly to it:

stinging
gold swarms
upon the spires
silver

    chants the litanies the
great bells are ringing with rose
the lewd fat bells

The poet avoided the obvious ideas that cluster around the subject of sunset: the timeworn meanings of silver and gold are freshened by the adroit combination of "stinging" and "swarms"; sound and image suggest the flight of a young queen and the creation of a new hive. "Spires" is echoed later in the poem in the phrase "a tall wind," and the poem concludes with an image of a dreamy sea. In an experiment Laura Riding and Robert Graves converted the pattern of this poem, the last part of which imitates a retreating wave, into conventional stanzas and concluded, rightly, that in the process the significance as well as the poetry was lost.

Informed critics, among them Barry A. Marks and the poet William Carlos Williams, have directed attention to "nonsun blob a" as probably the most difficult of Cummings' poems and yet as one containing very useful clues for the reader. It has a regularity of stanza, an Elizabethan tone, and a simplicity that might place it among the poet's charming verses for children. However, it offers a severe challenge to the mind: to put away old habits of associative thinking and to examine each stanza, line by line and word by word, for the relationships the poet has evoked. It also sums up Cummings' innovations and ideas to a remarkable degree. The emphasis Cummings himself placed upon it is evident in its position as the opening poem of the volume *One Times One.*

nonsun blob a
cold to

skylessness
sticking fire

my are your
are birds our all
and one gone
away the they

leaf of ghosts some
few creep there
here or on
unearth

Here the senses become elements of thought and the emotions are objectified to an extreme degree. The first stanza has neither verb nor expected sequences nor is it broken up to be reassembled, like an anagram. Each word compresses experiences from years of winter days; it is demanded of the reader that he be alert at all points so he may follow the clues in this celebration of bare, daunting specifics of a northern winter. Look at a winter sky: sunlessness is its chief characteristic but there is a gray waver, a "blob," sending out an almost invisible shine. The closing line, "sticking fire"—in which some critics observe a sexual connotation—brings into focus a dumb fear of being lost in a glacial world and paradoxically suggests all the physical and moral efforts to bring life-giving warmth to man, from Prometheus to nuclear industrial activities.

As we move on to a consideration of the second stanza, an observation made by Marks in his *E. E. Cummings* is especially illuminating. He noted: "the words of the first two lines . . . form two mathematical equations. One says, 'my + your = our.' The other, based on the phonetic pun, 'our' and 'are,' says, 'my = your'; 'my + your = birds'; 'my + your + birds = all.'" Intimations of what concerned Cummings—that the nature of unity is love—occur in the merging of the possessive pronouns: "mine" into "yours" into "ours" into "all." This unity is felt on repeated readings of the poem. But a Cummings poem is always in motion; the second stanza ends with the unity destroyed, the bird flock scattered in quest of a vanished leader.

The "a" which ends the first line of the poem is significant for an understanding of the third stanza. In its isolation it is related to autumn leaves creeping like crippled birds on a cold earth as indifferent as the cold sky recorded in the third stanza. Unfriendliness deprives the earth of its nourishing function; therefore Cummings used the prefix *un-* to modify the word *earth.* What is to be made of a typical Cummings inversion: "leaf of ghosts"? A remnant of birds or leaves in the increasing cold is described in the first stanza; later, birds reduced to creeping are non-birds, and cold earth is heartless as cold sky; both environments when deprived of their function as givers and nourishers, and therefore of their reality, are also ghosts. What Henry James called "perception at the pitch of passion" is involved in this "circular" poem. The implication is that of Greek tragedy: the helplessness of the alive, be it leaf or bird or a man and a woman. Yet there is joy in the contemplation of the real: a sun so clouded it may have burned out centuries ago; the relationship between the afflicted birds, leaves, and lovers—and the reader of the poem. Cummings, keeping his agonies to himself, nearly always ends on a note of joy.

This poem in twelve lines anticipates the essence of the nine stanzas of a later poem, "rosetree,rosetree" (*95 Poems*). The last stanza of "rosetree,rosetree" tells us again what the poet believes and hopes for:

lovetree!least the
rose alive must three,must
four and(to quite become
nothing)five times,proclaim
fate isn't fatal
—a heart her each petal

The reader may wonder why this master of experimental form chose rhymed stanzas for this piece. It is another instance of Cummings' sensitivity to choice among the formalities – an Elizabethan song brimming with transcendental ideas although the rose is a literal rose in a sizzle of bees. Traditional form attracts simple ideas: tree-bird, mob-war, flower-death-love. In this poem it serves as a counterweight to the complex ideas of a mystic, the poet "dreaming-true." Norman Friedman in a reasoned study of 175 worksheets of "rosetree,rosetree," rescued by Marion Morehouse Cummings from the usual destruction of preliminary work, reveals Cummings as a craftsman perfecting his materials over a long period of time. Throughout the 54 lines of the poem – in the adjustment of negative to positive, the victory in the final stanza over darkness and fatality – the cerebral element is always in play.

A poem that relates to this one – by melodic form and a transformation of abstracts so that they are vivid images – is the remarkable "what if a much of a which of a wind" (*One Times One*). Its rhythm perhaps reflects the influence of a ballad (attributed to Thomas Campion) which begins with "What if a day or a month or a year." But there the similarity ends. In the Cummings poem we have a deeply felt comment on the plight of universal life – nature and man – communicated by pairs of opposites: "gives the truth to summer's lie"; "when skies are hanged and oceans drowned,/ the single secret will still be man." In this "song" there are combinations that are reminiscent of Cummings' intriguing phrase "the square root of minus one" which he employed in at least three different contexts, notably in the Introduction to his *Collected Poems* where he wrote: "Mostpeople have less in common with ourselves than the squarerootofminusone." When he says, "Blow soon to never and never to twice/(blow life to isn't:blow death to was)/ – all nothing's only our hugest home," he has made eloquent poetry of his abstract idea.

William Troy has commented that certain pages of Cummings' Russian travel journal, *Eimi*, are as good as all but the best of his poetry. Certainly there is a relation between the prose and poetry in theme and technique.

In *Eimi* Cummings' words are positioned logistically to establish the impact of viewing Lenin's tomb. Others had written, according to their political bias, of that tomb. Cummings presented what his senses reported: the smells and sounds of the never-ending line of humanity descending into the bowels of the earth to get a glimpse of the corpse of a small man with a small face, their Messiah – as secret in death as he was in life. Cummings had gone to Russia to find out what the socialistic experiment was doing to help man toward being more alive. He found men and women with "a willingness not to live, if only they were allowed not to die," in John Peale Bishop's words. In some circumstances apathy is a means of survival but for the poet this was too little – or so it seemed to the young man of Harvard and New Hampshire. Vivid, even gay, portraits of Russians lighten the record but the following passage – illustrative of his firming style, that "specialization of sensibility" – is what he understood at Lenin's tomb:

facefacefaceface
  hand-
        fin-
            claw
  foot-
        hoof
  (tovarich)
            es to number of numberlessness (un
  -smiling)
  with dirt's dirt dirty dirtier with others' dirt with dirt of themselves

> dirtiest waitstand dirtily never smile shufflebudge dirty pausehalt
> Smilingless.

Francis Fergusson has referred to this passage as the beginning of "a sleepwalking death-rite." Cummings' deliberate abandonment of conventional syntax, which is based on an arrangement of thoughts and sensations already completed, makes the "instantaneous alone . . . his concern," as Troy put it, and he takes the reader into "an unworld of unmen lying in unsleep on an unbed of preternatural nullity."

Sensory awareness has been a dominant theme of Cummings' work discussed so far. A second primary theme in his work, both poetry and prose, is the integrity of the individual. The last lines of a sophisticated little poem about a Jewish tailor in Greenwich Village, "i say no world" (*50 Poems*), put his view succinctly: "unsellable not buyable alive/ one i say human being)one/ goldberger." Beginning with *The Enormous Room* and *Tulips and Chimneys,* Cummings celebrated individuals, perceiving the transcendental under the ephemeral disguise. Some of his poem portraits focused on the famous: Buffalo Bill ("Buffalo Bill's/ defunct," *Tulips and Chimneys*), the tragicomic dancer Jimmy Savo ("so little he is," in "New Poems" of *Collected Poems*), Picasso ("Picasso/ you give us Things," *XLI Poems*). In others he turned a clear but sympathetic eye on burlesque queens, circus clowns, "niggers dancing," the Greenwich Village "Professor Seagull." He wrote too of bums — and caught the spirit of their search for a "self" even as they scoured the gutters for a cigarette butt.

It follows that anything threatening individuality would be the object of his hatred. War, for example:

> you know what i mean when
> the first guy drops you know
> everybody feels sick or

> when they throw in a few gas
> and the oh baby shrapnel
> or my feet getting dim freezing or
> up to your you know what in water or
> with the bugs crawling right all up
> all everywhere over you all . . .

In these lines from "lis/-ten" (*Is 5*) Cummings conveys – through the agonized, almost hysterical, words of a soldier who was there – his deep-felt indignation against the senseless destruction of individuals. And the poet's skill transforms the ephemeral statistic of a newspaper battle account into transcendental man.

The threats to the integrity of the individual posed by a mechanized society are many and pervasive. "Progress is a comfortable disease," commented Cummings in "pity this busy monster,-manunkind" (*One Times One*), but a disease nonetheless. The attempts of man to identify with his inventions – to become the turbines and computers he developed – stir Cummings to remark: "A world of made/ is not a world of born." And so "when man determined to destroy/ himself he picked the was/ of shall and finding only why/ smashed it into because" ("when god decided to invent," *One Times One*).

In the morality *Santa Claus* Cummings speaks sharply against the blighting forces that keep a man from knowing his spontaneous self. "Knowledge has taken love out of the world/ and all the world is empty empty empty . . . joyless joyless joyless." The Child in the morality, however, can "truly see," as in Hans Christian Andersen's story "The Emperor's New Clothes." And when the Woman calls for death and Santa dressed as Death enters, she sees through the disguise because she looks with the eyes of the heart. Ironies of belief and unbelief are frequent in *Santa Claus*; the interchange of mask and costume is reminiscent of Shakespeare, and even more of the melodramatics of tent shows that toured the hinterland of the United States, and these again are related to the commedia dell'arte which began as skits performed on a wooden cart pulled by a donkey — to amuse Italian peasants. Cummings, writing to Allen Tate in 1946, said that the whole aim of *Santa Claus* was to make man remove his death mask, thereby becoming what he truly is: a human being.

In his concern to remove the death mask Cummings often employed satire. The satirist, it has been said, needs both irreverence and moral conviction. Cummings had both. His satire is like that of Swift; it comes from conviction that something is awry, as when he declared that this world is all aleak and "i'd rather learn from one bird how to sing/ than teach ten thousand stars how not to dance" ("New Poems," *Collected Poems*).

In the successful satires the penetration is trenchant, underlined by a cheerful ribaldry. At other times his intention is mislaid in a junk pile of name calling and irrelevant detail. Indignation sometimes results in an absence of poetic statement and a series of stereotypes. As Philip Horton has noted, Cummings is at times guilty of bad puns and satires that miss their mark ("a myth is as good as a smile" from "little joe gould"; "obey says toc,submit says tic,/ Eternity's a Five Year Plan" from "Jehovah buried,Satan dead," both in *No Thanks*). However, in a notable example of the satiric, "A Foreword to Krazy" (1946; collected in *A Miscellany*), Cummings explained the symbolism of George Herriman's comic-strip characters and at the same time he defined his own position as a satirist. The cast is made up of Ignatz Mouse, a brick-throwing cynic, Offissa Pupp, a sentimental policeman-dog, and the heroine, "slightly resembling a child's drawing of a cat." On the political level Offissa Pupp represents the "will of socalled society" while Ignatz Mouse is the destructive element. The benevolent overdog and the malevolent undermouse, as Cummings saw it, misunderstood Krazy Kat. Not only is she a symbol of an ideal democracy but she is personal — she transforms the brick into a kiss; the senses aided by the spirit produce joy.

These ideas ran counter to those expressed in T. S. Eliot's essay "Tradition and the Individual Talent" which for so long after its publication made the personal in literature suspect. But the swing of the pendulum through the centuries from the formalized prosaic (classic) to the formalized romantic is always rectifying the errors of critics. Today, such poets as John Berryman and Robert Lowell are carrying on experiments in the personal that Cummings would have found in his vein.

In two poems, "anyone lived in a pretty how town" and "my father moved through dooms of love" (both in *50 Poems*), Cummings very effectively worked the personal into a universal application. He used for one a contemplative narration of ideal lovers and for the other a portrait of the ideal man. The maturity of the poet's insights is displayed by his bold use of regular, rhymed stanzas to control a considered emotion and to weld it to his opinions, now sufficiently explored, of the social dilemma. The refrains are a charming blend of nursery rhyme ("sun moon stars rain" and "with up so floating many bells down") and sophisticated observation ("My father moved through theys of we").

Barry Marks has pointed out that as contemporary painters (like Juan Gris and Picasso) ambiguously employed a single curve for the neck of a vase and the edge of a guitar, so Cummings often deranged his syntax in order that a single word would both intensify a statement and question its validity; an example is the "how" in "anyone lived in a pretty how town." This word suggests, among other things, that the townspeople ask how and why about things from an emptiness of mind and an incapacity for simultaneity and the intuitive grasp. The direct vision of the painter-poet is similar to a child's delight in believing that a rain puddle is the ocean; it is a transcendental conception.

In the pretty how town "anyone" and "noone" are lovers; they live and love and die in a landscape of changing seasons, among children growing into adults and forgetting the realities and adults, "both little and small," without love or interest in life—from Cummings' penetrative view. The lively series of contrasts reinforces the ballad form; emotion and thought are strictly held to the development of the charade: "anyone" versus "someones," the individual opposed to the anxious status-seekers who "sowed their isn't" and "reaped their same." Children guessed the goodness of love between anyone and noone, because children are close to the intuitive life, but living things grow by imitation, so the children forgot as they imitated their "someones."

In the last line of the third stanza, "that noone loved him more by more," the word "noone" is emphasizing the public indifference as well as providing the identification of the "she" in the next stanza:

> when by now and tree by leaf
> she laughed his joy she cried his grief
> bird by snow and stir by still
> anyone's any was all to her

A compression of meanings is achieved in "when by now," "bird by snow," "tree by leaf," and they in turn are manipulated by repetitions suggested by later rhyme and alliteration: "all by all and deep by deep/ and more by more . . ." The climax of the ballad is in the line "and noone stooped to kiss his face." In the second to the last stanza the poet states the triumph of the individual way of life, as the lovers go hand in hand into eternity:

> noone and anyone earth by april
> wish by spirit and if by yes

Cummings' testament for his father, "my father moved through dooms of love," is a ballad only by stanza and innerly varied refrain; intertwined are seasonal references, as in "septembering arms of year extend" which gives individuality to the general term "harvest." It is heroic by virtue of lines that paraphrase the Prophets: "his anger was as right as rain/ his pity was as green as grain." The poem is distinguished by some fine couplets: "and should some why completely weep/ my father's fingers brought her sleep," and "if every friend became his foe/ he'd laugh and build a world with snow," which describes pretty accurately the poet himself. There is no narrative as such but the poem is held together by the feeling of compassion toward humble or unfortunate people.

In contrast to the abstract quality of "my father moved through dooms of love," a sequence of colorful details characterizes an early poem for Cummings' mother, "if there are any heavens" (*ViVa*). The opening lines establish clearly the heroic light in which Cummings viewed this woman who said of herself after a remarkable recovery from an automobile accident, "I'm tough":

> if there are any heavens my mother will(all by herself)have
> one. It will not be a pansy heaven nor
> a fragile heaven of lilies-of-the-valley but
> it will be a heaven of blackred roses

Cummings' virtuosity in the management of his mechanics may especially be noted in several poems revealing his intense concern with the individual. In one, the free-form poem beginning "5/ derbies-with-men-in-them" (*XLI Poems*), the reader is presented with a charade. With the poet he has entered a café that, like the Englishman's pub, seems more a social club than a restaurant: the customers play games such as backgammon and read and discuss the news while drinking coffee. Identity of place is established in the fourth stanza when one of the customers buys the Bawstinamereekin from a paperboy. But Cummings builds up an un-Yankee atmosphere with carefully chosen details: the men smoke Helmar cigarettes, one of them uses the word "effendi" and "swears in persian," two speak in Turkish, an Armenian record is played on the phonograph. This is, then, a Near Eastern café in Boston. Far from the feuds of the Old Country, proprietor and customers are united by homesickness. The men are not named; instead Cummings identifies them by lowercase letters:

a has gold
teeth b pink
suspenders c
reads Atlantis

And x beats y at backgammon. This device permits Cummings both to control his flood of feeling for the men and to stress their brotherhood. When two of them – the man with the gold teeth and the winner at backgammon – leave, Cummings says "exeunt ax"; and the coupled "by" follow. Cummings' characteristic use of space and capitals to underscore meaning is also to be found in this poem: "the pho/ nographisrunn/ ingd o w, n" and then "stopS."

Capital letters (not meant to be pronounced) serve as an organizing and emphasizing device in "sonnet entitled how to run the world)" (*No Thanks*), which begins:

A always don't there B being no such thing
for C can't casts no shadow D drink and

E eat of her voice in whose silence the music of spring
lives F feel opens but shuts understand
G gladly forget little having less

with every least each most remembering
H highest fly only the flag that's furled

Here we have a commentary on the existence of "mostpeople." This satire on the "unworld" employs the comparatives "less" and "least" to emphasize the triviality and sterility of that world, while the clause "in whose silence the music of spring/ lives" indicates what, for Cummings, is one of the symbols of the real world, the transcendental world. There is a flash of mocking humor in the repetition of the pedantic "entitled" in the ninth line of the poem, "(sestet entitled grass is flesh . . ." but even this line has a serious purpose: to reinforce the idea of a world where people merely exist. It is followed by a richly thought-provoking statement, "any dream/ means more than sleep as more than know means guess)," which prepares the way for the masterly concluding line, "children building this rainman out of snow." In this poem Cummings uses for the most part simple words but combines them so that the repetitions and contrasts of sound add a fresh dimension to the theme and subtly contribute to the feeling of empathy evoked for the individuals trapped in the "unworld."

Where in these two poems Cummings used, variously, lowercase and capital letters as controlling devices, in "there are 6 doors" (*ViVa*), it is repetition of the phrase "next door" that governs the orderly sequence. "Next door(but four)" lives a whore with "a multitude of chins"; "next door/ but three" a ghost "Who screams Faintly" is the tenant and "next/ Door but two" a man and his wife who "throw silently things/ Each at other." Then Cummings tells what happens to some men who have been jettisoned by society:

> ,next door but One
> a on Dirty bed Mangy from person Porous
> sits years its of self fee(bly
> Perpetually coughing And thickly spi)tting

Finally, "next door nobody/ seems to live at present . . . or,bedbugs." The reader is left to ponder several kinds of waste of human life. Emerson wrote in his essay "Self-Reliance," "This one fact the world hates, that the soul *becomes*"; Cummings recorded in poem after poem instances of the world preventing the action of the soul – but with the purpose of rousing the transcendental spirit latent in his readers.

The individuals pictured in "mortals)" (*50 Poems*) are very different from those in the rooms "next door" and so are the technical devices used. Cummings here turns to highly skilled acrobats and puts them into motion on the page:

mortals)

climbi
ng i
nto eachness begi
n
dizzily
swingthings
of speeds of
trapeze gush somersaults
open ing
hes shes
&meet&
swoop
fully is are ex
quisite theys of re
turn
a
n
d
fall which now drop who all dreamlike

(im

"Eachness" is a critical word in this poem: as George Haines IV has pointed out, the individuality of the performers is emphasized by the separation of "climbi" and "begi" from the end letters "ng" and "n"; the swinging of the trapeze is in the line repetition "of speeds of." The reader discovering a similar pattern in "&meet&" by this time is responding with a jump of his muscles, as occurs in watching ballet or circus. As the "fully" continues into "is are ex," movement has entered the area of the unknown; the symbol *x* ("ex") is equal to the mystery of the encounters of the "is" and "are," the "hes" and "shes." The use of "a/ n/ d" permits visualization of the trapeze. The fortunate climax of "who all dreamlike" brings together the specific skills and the hovering mystery of art, whose function is to redeem what otherwise would vanish from the earth like a dream. In another sense, the acrobats are a congruent image since even the most skilled is in peril at every performance (mortals, Cummings called them) yet they are completely and happily themselves in the exercise of their art. From the final line to the first one in this "circular" poem—"im" plus "mortal"—the poet justifies his contention that precision makes motion which makes life, and that the "dark beginnings are his luminous ends."

Why did Cummings choose the symbol of acrobats for a metaphysical statement? He may have been inspired, as was Rilke, by "Les Saltimbanques" of Picasso. More likely, his enjoyment of folk amusements dictated the vehicle for his fundamental belief: mortals, by devotion to a skill, an art, become immortal.

Before leaving this aspect of Cummings' work, we may appropriately turn back to his prose to find a revealing conjunction of theme and technique. In *The Enormous Room* Cummings had used a phrase of John Bunyan's, the "Delectable Mountains," to refer to certain individuals—physically mistreated, spiritually mutilated, and yet triumphantly overcoming their situations. Of one example, whom he christened The Zulu, he said, "His angular anatomy expended and collected itself with an effortless spontaneity . . . But he was more. There are certain things in which one is unable to believe for the simple reason that he never ceases to feel them. Things of this sort—things which are always inside of us and in fact are us and which consequently will not be pushed off or away where we can begin thinking about them—are no longer things; they, and the us which they are, equals A Verb; an IS. The Zulu, then, I must perforce call an IS." Thus, using one of his typical devices, substitution of one part of speech for another, Cummings converted one way of seeing and of thinking into another to emphasize a theme that would be meshed in all of his writing. Whenever *is*, the verb, is turned into a noun, it becomes even more of a verb; it is dramatized, it gains—as Lloyd Frankenberg put it—the force of the colloquial "He *is* somebody." In other words, the quality of being becomes an active principle, the individual becomes a whole person, responding to the totality of experience.

A third major theme in Cummings' work, already touched upon, is the revelation of what it means *truly* to love. In his experiments with the idea of love Cummings assigned to the word the multiple connotations inherent in it: sexual, romantic, platonic. The most intense love, paradoxically, must function with the greatest objectivity; subjective impressions must be corrected by intent observation of objects, human or otherwise. Dante could write of his ideal Lady; Cummings addressed to a platonic vision a bawdy valentine that is revelatory of his stance toward life and art ("on the Madam's best april the," *Is 5*).

In the era following World War I and acceleration of industrial growth, disregard of an earlier generation's restraints on sex became a means of protesting against the increased restrictions of the national life. In literature, Sherwood Anderson, Ernest Hemingway, Eugene O'Neill, and Henry Miller emphasized the necessity for sexual freedom. Cummings participated in this critique of the dehumanizing forces dominating the modern scene. Frankly rejoicing in sexuality as a nourishing element in an integrated life, a bond between man and the cosmos, or satirizing customs based on habit and fear of public opinion, he wrote "O sweet spontaneous" (*Tulips and Chimneys*) and "she being Brand" (*Is 5*) and "i will be/ Moving in the Street of her" (*And*). A poem on Sally Rand, "out of a supermetamathical subpreincestures"

(*No Thanks*), is not only a celebration of the fan dancer of the 1930's but also a transcendental view of the wonder of life. And it is a significant contrast to "raise the shade/ will youse dearie?" (*And*), a realistic piece exposing the joylessness in the pursuit of "pleasure."

Cummings eventually went "beyond sex as a critique of society and . . . beyond self-indulgence to self-discipline based on a new understanding of love," as Barry Marks put it. Cummings believed that morality depends on whether there is genuine giving on both sides. Sexuality is an ingredient of any I-you relationship, in the impersonal way that there is a trace of sugar in all vegetable and animal tissues, even if they taste salty or bitter. He illustrated insights into giving in a philosophical poem, "(will you teach a/ wretch to live/ straighter than a needle)," and in a comment on poverty that moves in nursery-rhyme couplets from realistic deprivations to a more desperate psychological dilemma, "if you can't eat you got to/ smoke and we ain't got/ nothing to smoke" (both in *50 Poems*). And a poem (from *No Thanks*) with neat stanzas to control his vehemence tells the reader from what a distance the poet has come, smiling in a wry wisdom:

> be of love(a little)
> More careful
> Than of everything
> guard her perhaps only
>
> . . . .
>
> (Dare until a flower,
> understanding sizelessly sunlight
> Open what thousandth why and
> discover laughing)

Lloyd Frankenberg, in his introduction to a London reprint of *One Times One*, said that, in effect, all of Cummings' poems were love poems. A neat summation but then an "anatomy" of love is also necessary. Conventional behavior in love is related to conventional punctuation in prosody. And for a poet who lived on the tips of not only his nerves but also his mind, love covers all of existence: in one aspect it is involved with spit on the sidewalk and in another with moonlight on the thighs of his lady; the value of a thing or an experience is its revelation of an involvement with life. Finally, in *95 Poems* and *73 Poems,* Cummings came to a position whose simplicity may have surprised him: a filial relation to the Divine. So this was what it meant, the witty comment he made on his own struggles in *Is 5*:

> since feeling is first
> who pays any attention
> to the syntax of things
> will never wholly kiss you;
>
> . . . .
>
> for life's not a paragraph
>
> And death i think is no parenthesis

In his critical studies T. S. Eliot repeated his view that the entire output of certain writers constitutes a single work similar to an epic (*The Divine Comedy* or Williams' *Paterson*) and that individual pieces are endowed with meaning by other pieces and by the whole context of the work. This view may assist to an understanding of Cummings: fragmentation dissolves in the continuity of recurrent themes; interrelated images and symbols by their organizing force reflect and echo each other with cumulative effect. Cummings would have said it more specifically: in the here and now we can be happy and immortal if we use our wits and our will. Even if evil and death are the co-kings of this world, love is my king, and in serving him is my joy.

It is a leap into faith when a man casts off the customary motives of humanity and ventures to trust himself as taskmaster; he will need courage and vision "that a simple purpose may be to him as strong as iron necessity is to others" — so Emerson thought. From *Tulips and Chimneys* to *Poems 1923–1954* — a constellation of refracted and repeated images — to the posthumous *73 Poems,* Cummings led a succession of readers to accept his declaration: "I have no sentimentality at all. If you haven't got that, you're not afraid to write of love and death."

The metaphysical cord on which Cummings' sonnets are threaded was in evidence in the early "a connotation of infinity/ sharpens the temporal splendor of this night" (*Tulips and Chimneys*), in "put off your faces,Death:for day is over" (*ViVa*), and in "Love/ coins His most gradual gesture,/ and whittles life to eternity" ("it is so long since my heart has been with yours," *Is 5*). The efficacy of love in its multiple aspects pervades the notions of death until death becomes a gate to life. Dying is a verb as opposed to a deathly noun: "forgive us the sin of death." In another early poem, "somewhere i have never travelled,gladly beyond/ any experience" (*ViVa*), the abstraction "spring" is personified and its essential mystery is presented through the adverbs *skilfully, mysteriously, suddenly,* used as in the later poetry are *miraculous, illimitable, immeasurable*: adjectival aspects of natural phenomena capable of being perceived but incapable of being truly labeled or measured.

The concern of Cummings, even in his Sitwellian phase, with juxtaposed improbables — locomotives with roses — was an effort to get at the quintessence of an apparently trivial subject. Its mystery could be reached successfully only by the evolution of devices he had scrupulously crafted. In his war against formal "thinking" he was not against study or ideas; it was an opposition to the conformity which the accumulation of "knowledge" is inclined to impose. To discover the true nature of the world — to know it; to act in it; for the artist, to depict it — is the Cummings metaphysic, his politics, and his aesthetic. The world of cyclical process is for him a timeless world. He does not deny either the past or the future; rather he denies that hope or regret should warp the living moment. In this way he is related to Coleridge and to Blake (related doubly to the latter by reason of his sensitive drawings, such as the celebrated sketch of Charlie Chaplin). His eyes are fixed on fulfillment, consenting to the perpetuation of life through death as in "rosetree,rosetree." The individual rose dies that a hundred roses may be born; true lovers will be reborn into perfect love.

The antithesis between the false routine world and the true world is seen with icy clarity by a poet who feels mortality sitting on his shoulder. The result is a complexity of vision. That it should have cost so much to get there does not trouble the poet of transcendence; he is a compeer of all seekers, including a tramp on the highway. A poet's function is to embody in a poem the dynamics of nature (including his own response) which is primarily a mystery. Heightened awareness leads to a new dimension that leads into transcendentalism supported by specific detail: in "luminous tendril of celestial wish" (*Xaipe*), the cyclical moon is regarded as evidence of process leading to death and rebirth; the poet's humility is indicated by "teach disappearing also me the keen/ illimitable secret of begin."

In *95 Poems* the poetic argument rises into an intense clarity. The affirmative transcending the negative as in "All lose,whole find" ("one's not half two," *One Times One*) and in "the most who die,the more we live" ("what if a much of a which of a wind," *One Times One*) has entered a final phase. The poet has now realized that the transcendental cannot abolish the "fact" of death but he proves the worth of the affirmative as the polarizing element of his philosophy. The former devices of making nouns into verbs and shifting the placement of antitheses are less in evidence; the reality of "appearances" is acknowledged: "now air is air and thing is thing:no bliss/ of heavenly earth beguiles our spirits,whose/ miraculously disenchanted eyes/ live the magnificent honesty of space." This is a reminder of the early "let's live suddenly without thinking/ under honest trees" (*And*). The poet, however, has come into the higher turn of the spiral of mystical development where the phenomenal world is transfigured and a tree is really understood.

In this volume Cummings has collected all of his phases: (1) look at what is happening around you; (2) the imagination is more real than reality; (3) the search for life and self brings you back to a transformed reality that is shared with a grasshopper on a flowering weed. As S. I. Hayakawa wrote in *Language in Thought and Action,* the only certainty and security is within the disciplined mind; so when Cummings says in "in time of daffodils(who know"

> and in a mystery to be
> (when time from time shall set us free)
> forgetting me,remember me

the troubadour is telling his lady to forget his life *in* time; to remember that his mortal love always looked toward lovers in immortality. Just so did his preoccupation with twilight reach beyond mist and the "dangerous first stars" to a world new to the senses.

Begin as you mean to go on. The English proverb may explain why the young Cummings was attracted to a statement of Keats: "I am certain of nothing but the holiness of the Heart's affections, and the truth of Imagination." The innovative devices that the young Cummings developed to implement this idea were a successful means of communication in the modern world. But the Cummings of *73 Poems* has traveled farther than that: into the realm of transcendence. The poet who said "—who'll solve the depths of horror to defend/a sunbeam's architecture with his life" ("no man, if men are gods," *One Times One*) has earned the right to explain time by timelessness. In total compassion he declares, in the last poem in *73 Poems*:

> (being forever born a foolishwise
> proudhumble citizen of ecstasies
> more steep than climb can time with all his years)
>
> he's free into the beauty of the truth;
>
> and strolls the axis of the universe
> —love. Each believing world denies, whereas
> your lover(looking through both life and death)
> timelessly celebrates the merciful
>
> wonder no world deny may or believe.

Growing from poem to poem — shedding skin after skin — Cummings emerges as really himself, and therefore as everyone: that is the true definition of transcendence. The artist's formalities have become clear as a washed windowpane, or the purity of a flower upturned to receive a heavenly dew — the canticles of a mystic.

Selected Bibliography

Works of E. E. Cummings

For convenience of reference the capitalization of book titles in this pamphlet follows conventional form rather than the typographical style of the title page in each book, which often reflected Cummings' own preference for lowercase letters.

Eight Harvard Poets: E. Estlin Cummings, S. Foster Damon, J. R. Dos Passos, Robert Hillyer, R. S. Mitchell, William A Norris, Dudley Poore, Cuthbert Wright. New York: Laurence J. Gomme, 1917. (Contains eight poems by Cummings.)

The Enormous Room. New York: Boni and Liveright, 1922.

Tulips and Chimneys. New York: Thomas Seltzer, 1923.

& (And). New York: Privately printed, 1925.

XLI Poems. New York: Dial Press, 1925.

Is 5. New York: Boni and Liveright, 1926.

Him. New York: Boni and Liveright, 1927.

Christmas Tree. New York: American Book Bindery, 1928.

[No title] New York: Covici, Friede, 1930.

CIOPW. New York: Covici, Friede, 1931.

W (ViVa). New York: Horace Liveright, 1931.

Eimi. New York: Covici, Friede, 1933.

No Thanks. New York: Golden Eagle Press, 1935.

Tom. New York: Arrow Editions, 1935.

1/20 (One Over Twenty). London: Roger Roughton, 1936.

Collected Poems. New York: Harcourt, Brace, 1938.

50 Poems. New York: Duell, Sloan and Pearce, 1940.

1 x 1 (One Times One). New York: Henry Holt, 1944.

Anthropos: The Future of Art. Mount Vernon, N.Y.: Golden Eagle Press, 1944.

Santa Claus: A Morality. New York: Henry Holt, 1946.

Puella Mea. Mount Vernon, N.Y.: Golden Eagle Press, 1949.

Xaipe. New York: Oxford University Press, 1950.

I: Six Nonlectures. Cambridge, Mass.: Harvard University Press, 1953.

Poems 1923–1954. New York: Harcourt, Brace, 1954.

E. E. Cummings: A Miscellany, edited by George J. Firmage. New York: Argophile Press, 1958.

95 Poems. New York: Harcourt, Brace, 1958.

100 Selected Poems. New York: Grove, 1959.
Selected Poems 1923–1958. London: Faber and Faber, 1960.
Adventures in Value, with photographs by Marion Morehouse. New York: Harcourt, Brace and World, 1962.
73 Poems. New York: Harcourt, Brace and World, 1963.
E. E. Cummings: A Miscellany Revised, edited by George J. Firmage. New York: October House, 1965.

Current American Reprints

E. E. Cummings: A Miscellany Revised, edited by George J. Firmage. New York: October House. $2.95.
E. E. Cummings: A Selection of Poems, with an introduction by Horace Gregory. New York: Harvest (Harcourt, Brace and World). $1.65.
E. E. Cummings: Three Plays and a Ballet (Him, Anthropos, Santa Claus, and *Tom),* edited with an introduction by George J. Firmage. New York: October House. $2.95.
Enormous Room, The. New York: Modern Library (Random House). $2.45.
Fifty Poems. New York: Universal Library (Grosset and Dunlap). $1.25.
I: Six Nonlectures. New York: Atheneum. $1.65.
100 Selected Poems. New York: Evergreen (Grove). $1.75.

Letters

Selected Letters of E. E. Cummings, edited by F. W. Dupee and George Stade. New York: Harcourt, Brace and World, 1969.

Bibliographies

Firmage, George J. *E. E. Cummings: A Bibliography.* Middletown, Conn.: Wesleyan University Press, 1960.
Lauter, Paul. *E. E. Cummings: Index to First Lines and Bibliography of Works by and about the Poet.* Denver: Alan Swallow, 1955.

Critical Comments and Studies

Abel, Lionel. "Clown or Comic Poet?" *Nation,* 140:749–50 (June 26, 1935).
Baum, S. V. "E. E. Cummings: The Technique of Immediacy," *South Atlantic Quarterly,* 53:70–88 (January 1954).
———, editor. *ΕΣΤΙ: E. E. Cummings and the Critics.* East Lansing: Michigan State University Press, 1962. (Good bibliography.)
Blackmur, R. P. "Notes on E. E. Cummings' Language," in *Language as Gesture.* New York: Harcourt, Brace, 1952. Pp. 317–40.

Selected Bibliography

Bode, Carl. "E. E. Cummings and Exploded Verse," in *The Great Experiment in American Literature.* New York: Praeger, 1961. Pp. 79–100.

Breit, Harvey. "The Case for the Modern Poet," *New York Times Magazine,* November 3, 1946, pp. 20, 58, 60–61.

———. "Talk with E. E. Cummings," *New York Times Book Review,* December 31, 1950, p. 10.

Deutsch, Babette. *Poetry in Our Time.* New York: Henry Holt, 1952. Pp. 111–18.

Dickey, James. "E. E. Cummings," in *Babel to Byzantium: Poets and Poetry Now.* New York: Farrar, Straus and Giroux, 1968. Pp. 100–6.

Fergusson, Francis. "When We Were Very Young," *Kenyon Review,* 12:701–5 (Autumn 1950).

Frankenberg, Lloyd. *Pleasure Dome: On Reading Modern Poetry.* Boston: Houghton Mifflin, 1949. Pp. 157–94.

Friedman, Norman. *E. E. Cummings: The Art of His Poetry.* Baltimore: Johns Hopkins Press, 1960.

———. *E. E. Cummings: The Growth of a Writer.* Carbondale: Southern Illinois University Press, 1964.

Haines, George, IV. "::2:1 – The World and E. E. Cummings," *Sewanee Review,* 59:206–27 (Spring 1951).

Harvard Wake, No. 5 (Spring 1946). (A special Cummings number.)

Hollander, John. "Poetry Chronicle," *Partisan Review,* 26:142–43 (Winter 1959).

Honig, Edwin. " 'Proud of His Scientific Attitude,' " *Kenyon Review,* 17:484–90 (Summer 1955).

Horton, Philip, and Sherry Mangan. "Two Views of Cummings," *Partisan Review,* 4:58–63 (May 1938).

Marks, Barry A. *E. E. Cummings.* New York: Twayne, 1964.

Moore, Marianne. "People Stare Carefully," *Dial,* 80:49–52 (January 1926).

———. "One Times One," in *Predilections.* New York: Viking, 1955. Pp. 140–43.

Munson, Gorham B. "Syrinx," *Secession,* No. 5 (July 1923), pp. 2–11.

Norman, Charles. *E. E. Cummings: The Magic-Maker.* New York: Macmillan, 1958.

Riding, Laura, and Robert Graves. *A Survey of Modernist Poetry.* London: Heinemann, 1927. Pp. 9–34.

Shapiro, Karl. *Essay on Rime.* New York: Reynal and Hitchcock, 1945. Pp. 20–21.

Sitwell, Edith. *Aspects of Modern Poetry.* London: Duckworth, 1934. Pp. 251–57.

Spencer, Theodore. "Technique as Joy," *Harvard Wake,* No. 5 (Spring 1946), pp. 25–29.

Tate, Allen. "E. E. Cummings," in *Reactionary Essays on Poetry and Ideas.* New York: Scribner's, 1936. Pp. 228–33.

Time, September 14, 1962. (A full-page obituary.)

Troy, William. "Cummings's Non-land of Un-," *Nation,* 136:413 (April 12, 1933).

Voisin, Laurence. "Quelques poètes américains," *Europe: Revue Mensuelle,* 37:36–37 (February–March 1959).

Von Abele, Rudolph. " 'Only to Grow': Change in the Poetry of E. E. Cummings," *PMLA,* 70:913–33 (December 1955).

Wegner, Robert E. *The Poetry and Prose of E. E. Cummings.* New York: Harcourt, Brace and World, 1965.

Williams, William Carlos. "E. E. Cummings' Paintings and Poems," *Arts Digest,* 29:7–8 (December 1, 1954).

Wilson, Edmund. "*Him,*" *New Republic,* 70:293–94 (November 2, 1927).